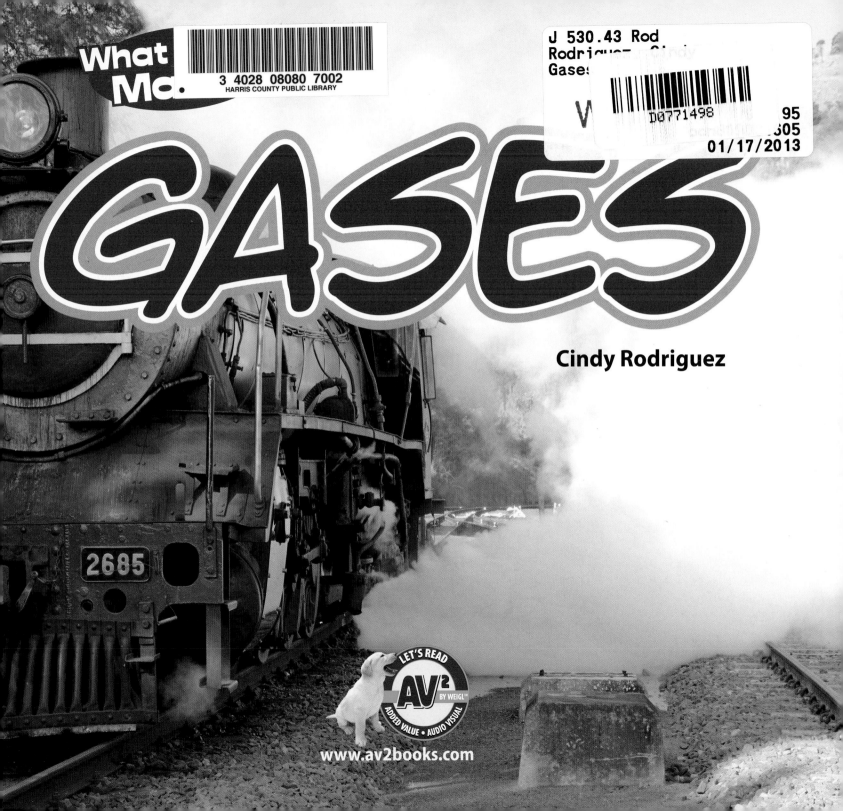

What Ma.

GASES

Cindy Rodriguez

LET'S READ
AV2 BY WEIGL
ADDED VALUE · AUDIO VISUAL

www.av2books.com

LET'S READ
AV²
BY WEIGL™
ADDED VALUE • AUDIO VISUAL

Go to **www.av2books.com**, and enter this book's unique code.

BOOK CODE

E 2 2 5 2 1 2

AV² by Weigl brings you media enhanced books that support active learning.

AV² provides enriched content that supplements and complements this book. Weigl's AV² books strive to create inspired learning and engage young minds in a total learning experience.

Your AV² Media Enhanced books come alive with...

Audio
Listen to sections of the book read aloud.

Video
Watch informative video clips.

Embedded Weblinks
Gain additional information for research.

Try This!
Complete activities and hands-on experiments.

Key Words
Study vocabulary, and complete a matching word activity.

Quizzes
Test your knowledge.

Slide Show
View images and captions, and prepare a presentation.

... and much, much more!

Published by AV² by Weigl
350 5th Avenue, 59th Floor New York, NY 10118
Website: www.av2books.com   www.weigl.com

Library of Congress Control Number: 2012942645

ISBN 978-1-61913-602-1 (hard cover)
ISBN 978-1-61913-604-5 (soft cover)

Printed in the United States of America in North Mankato, Minnesota
1 2 3 4 5 6 7 8 9   16 15 14 13 12

062012
WEP170512

Editor: Aaron Carr   Design: Mandy Christiansen

Weigl acknowledges Getty Images, iStock, and Dreamstime as image suppliers for this title.

GASES

What is Matter?

CONTENTS

3

Gases have no size.

Gases have no shape.

The air you breathe is a gas.

Gases can spread to fill a big space.

Gases can pack to fit a small space.

Gases fill their containers.

Gases can be many colors.

Some gases can not be seen.

Balloons and bubbles are filled with gas.

Gases can move.

Moving gases can be felt.

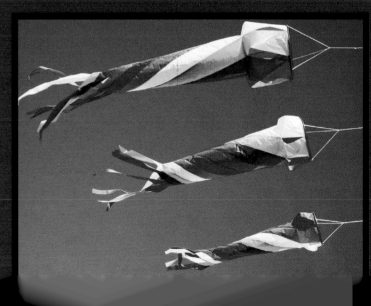

Wind is moving air.

Gases are one kind of matter.

Solids and liquids
are other kinds of matter.

There are many gases, solids, and liquids.

Gases turn to liquids when they get cold.

This is called condensation.

Condensation can make water form on glass.

Liquids turn to gases when they get hot.

This is called boiling.

Water turns to steam when it boils.

The Sun heats the air.

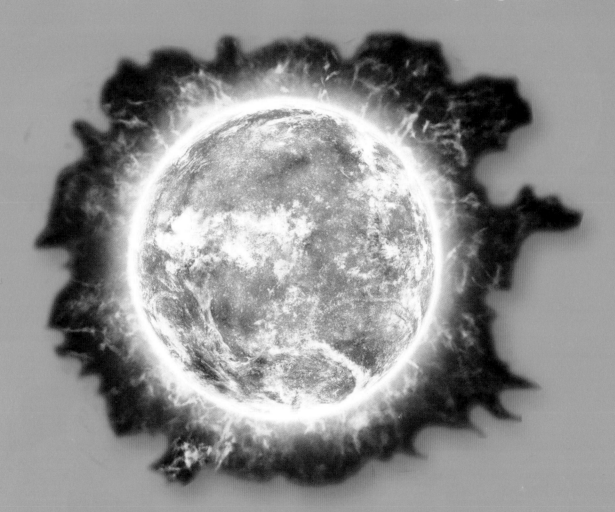

This heat turns water into a gas.

The Sun helps turn water to clouds, mist, and steam.

Water is an important kind of matter.

Water can be a gas, solid, or liquid.

Many things
are made of water.

Everything around you is made of matter.
Which of these things is a gas?
Are any of these things solids or liquids?

Are any of these gases condensing or boiling?

23

KEY WORDS

Research has shown that as much as 65 percent of all written material published in English is made up of 300 words. These 300 words cannot be taught using pictures or learned by sounding them out. They must be recognized by sight. This book contains 43 common sight words to help young readers improve their reading fluency and comprehension. This book also teaches young readers several important content words. These words are paired with pictures to aid in learning and improve understanding.

Page	Sight Words First Appearance	Page	Content Words First Appearance
4	a, air, have, is, no, the, you	4	gases, shape, size
6	big, can, small, their, to	6	containers, space
8	and, are, be, many, not, some, with	8	balloons, bubbles, colors
10	move	10	wind
12	kind, of, one, other, there	12	liquids, matter, solids
14	get, make, on, they, this, water, when	14	condensation, glass
18	helps, into	16	boiling, steam
20	an, important, made	18	clouds, heat, mist, Sun
22	any, around, these, things, which, you	22	everything

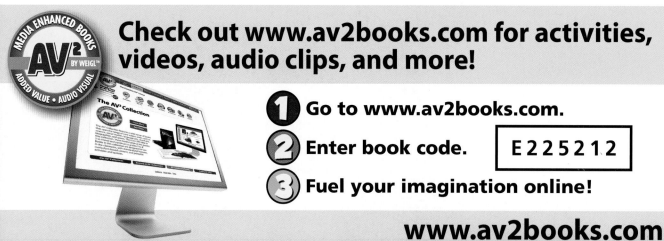

Check out www.av2books.com for activities, videos, audio clips, and more!

1 Go to www.av2books.com.

2 Enter book code. E 2 2 5 2 1 2

3 Fuel your imagination online!

www.av2books.com

24